Suited for SUCCESS

Suited for SUCCESS

Cathy Duplantis

JESSE DUPLANTIS MINISTRIES
Destrehan, LA

Unless otherwise identified, Scripture quotations are taken from the King James Version.

Scripture quotations taken from the Amplified® Bible (AMPC), Copyright © 1954, 1958, 1962, 1964, 1965, 1987 by The Lockman Foundation Used by permission. www.lockman.org.

Scripture quotations taken from the (NASB®) New American Standard Bible®, Copyright © 1960, 1971, 1977, 1995, by The Lockman Foundation. Used by permission. All rights reserved. www.lockman.org.

Scripture quotations marked (NLT) are taken from the Holy Bible, New Living Translation, copyright ©1996, 2004, 2015 by Tyndale House Foundation. Used by permission of Tyndale House Publishers, Carol Stream, Illinois 60188. All rights reserved.

Scripture quotations marked TPT are from The Passion Translation®. Copyright © 2017, 2018, 2020 by Passion & Fire Ministries, Inc. Used by permission. All rights reserved. ThePassionTranslation.com.

Suited for Success
© Copyright 2023—Cathy Duplantis

Published by Cathy Duplantis
PO Box 1089
Destrehan, LA 70047
www.jdm.org

All rights reserved. No portion of this book may be reproduced, stored in a retrieval system, or transmitted in any form or by any means—electronic, mechanical, photocopy, recording, scanning, or other—except for brief quotations in critical reviews or articles, without the prior written permission of the publisher.

Printed in the United States of America.

ISBN 13: 978-1-63416-807-6

1 2 3 4 5 6 7 8 9 | 28 27 26 25 24 23

CONTENTS

CHAPTER 1
Suited for Success 1

CHAPTER 2
The Curse Has Been Reversed 7

CHAPTER 3
Bankrupt the Devil! 15

CHAPTER 4
It's Time for You to THRIVE 23

CHAPTER 5
Take the Path to the Good Life 31

CHAPTER 6
Empowered to Prosper 39

CHAPTER 7
God's Reward System 47

CHAPTER 8
Destined for Success 53

CHAPTER 9
Turn Your Nothing into Something 59

CHAPTER 10
God Wants You to Succeed 63

CHAPTER 11
Beware of the Dream Killers 69

PRAYER OF SALVATION 81
ABOUT THE AUTHOR 83
OTHER BOOKS BY CATHY DUPLANTIS 85

CHAPTER 1

Suited for SUCCESS

Success: Many people get upset when a Christian seeks it, but success is not a bad word. In fact, the first time it was used in the Bible was by God to Joshua after the death of Moses.

In the first chapter of Joshua, verses eight and nine, God said, *"This book of the law shall not depart out of thy mouth; but thou shalt meditate therein day and night, that thou mayest observe to do according to all that is written therein: for then thou shalt make thy way prosperous, and then thou shalt have good success. Have not I commanded thee? Be strong and of a good courage; be not afraid, neither be thou dismayed: for the LORD thy God is with thee whithersoever thou goest."*

Joshua must have had concerns about stepping into Moses' shoes as leader of Israel. Wouldn't you? After all, Moses was the long-awaited deliverer, miracle-worker, and the man that spoke face to face with God. But now God was speaking to Joshua and telling him how to succeed. And just like it was with Joshua, so it is with us today: Prosperity and success are always a direct result of following God's Word.

I believe that wisdom and knowledge from God's Word can enable each of us to advance to the top regardless of obstacles or recessions. When you need favor, wisdom, protection, or prosperity, God's Word shows you how to pray effectively and receive it. If sickness attacks your body, you can apply God's Word and receive your healing. No matter where you go or what you come into contact with, you can be victorious. Or as we say in South Louisiana, "If you fall in an outhouse, you come out smelling like a rose."

Equipped with Essentials

God wants you to be a success and has provided you with the essentials you need to succeed in this life. You see, His plan of salvation includes more than just eternal life and a mansion in Heaven. As a member of the family of God, you have access to benefits that provide for everything you could ever need in this life.

In fact, the moment you were born again, you were issued a suit of armor designed by God Himself. From the top of your head to the soles of your feet, you are equipped with supernatural clothing that is impenetrable by the enemy. I like to think of it as my success suit.

Ephesians, chapter six, describes it this way:

Finally, my brethren, be strong in the Lord, and in the power of His might.

Put on the whole armour of God, that ye may be able to stand against the wiles of the devil.

For we wrestle not against flesh and blood, but against principalities, against powers, against the rulers of the darkness of this world, against spiritual wickedness in high places.

Wherefore take unto you the whole armour of God, that ye may be able to withstand in the evil day, and having done all, to stand.

Stand therefore, having your loins girt about with truth, and having on the breastplate of righteousness;

And your feet shod with the preparation of the Gospel of peace;

Above all, taking the shield of faith, wherewith ye shall be able to quench all the fiery darts of the wicked.

And take the helmet of salvation, and the sword of the Spirit, which is the Word of God.

EPHESIANS 6:10-17

Have you ever tried to dress a child that is distracted or refuses to help while you are dressing them? It can be very frustrating. But when that same child is excited about going somewhere, they will tear off their pajamas, throw on their play clothes, and look for someone to help with the buttons and laces. Big difference!

God has provided this awesome suit of armor so that you can successfully *"stand against the wiles of the devil."* But it can't help you unless you wear it. It is your responsibility to accept it and put it on. Romans 13:12 tells us, *"The night is far spent, the day is at hand: let us therefore cast off the works of darkness, and let us put on the armour of light."*

How do you do that? You read God's Word and accept it by faith. You meditate on it day and night and don't let it depart from your mouth. Follow God's instructions to Joshua and you will be a success going somewhere to happen. You will be suited for success and equipped with the essentials for victory!

Accessorize Your Faith

Once you are suited with God's armor, you can browse through His Word for ways to accessorize your success suit. Second Peter 1:4-8 says,

> *Whereby are given unto us exceeding great and precious promises: that by these ye might be partakers of the divine nature, having escaped the corruption that is in the world through lust.*
> *And beside this, giving all diligence, **add to your faith** virtue; and to virtue knowledge;*
> *And to knowledge temperance; and to temperance patience; and to patience godliness;*
> *And to godliness brotherly kindness; and to brotherly kindness charity.*
> *For if these things be in you, and abound, they make you that ye shall neither be barren nor unfruitful in the knowledge of our Lord Jesus Christ.*

What an awesome promise! You have been given exceeding great and precious promises. You are a partaker of the divine nature. You have not only been given the measure of faith (Romans 12:3), but, according to this passage, you can accessorize your faith—by adding virtue, knowledge, temperance, patience, godliness, brotherly kindness, and love (charity). When these things are in your life, you will be productive, fruitful, and will bring glory to God.

Take Time for a Closer Look

Mirrors are wonderful things. If you take the time to use them, they will reveal things that need to be fixed and save you from embarrassing situations. You will be able to see the lettuce in your teeth, the ketchup on your cheek, or the stain on your tie. But, most importantly, it will reveal the hem of your skirt inside your pantyhose! But you have to look in the mirror or else you will be exposed.

That's what happened to me years ago. The bathroom of the church I was visiting did not have a full-length mirror, so I just moved my hand down the back of my skirt to make sure everything was in place. The skirt that I was wearing had a lining and two layers of peach chiffon, so I did not realize that everything except the top outer sheer layer was inside my pantyhose. I walked all the way up the aisle of the church to the front pew before someone told me what had happened. Since that time, I have come to understand how important it is to take time for a closer look in the mirror before heading out the door.

The point? Don't take things for granted. The Word of God is your mirror, and before you begin anything, always take time for a closer look and allow it to reveal things that you may need to adjust. James 1:23-25 says, *"For if any be a hearer of the Word, and not a doer, he is like unto a man beholding his natural face in a glass: For he beholdeth himself, and goeth his way, and straightway forgetteth what manner of man he was. But whoso looketh into the perfect law of liberty, and continueth therein, he being not a forgetful hearer, but a doer of the work, this man shall be blessed in his deed."*

God's Word will reveal the way for you to succeed. Second Timothy 2:15 (AMPC) says, *"Study and be eager and do your utmost to present yourself to God approved (tested by trial), a workman who has no cause to be ashamed, correctly analyzing and accurately dividing [rightly handling and skillfully teaching] the Word of Truth."* When you are diligent to study God's Word and do what it says, you will never be ashamed. You will know where to go and what to do when you get there. You will be blessed and fully suited for success.

CHAPTER 2

The Curse Has Been REVERSED

Curse: that word never would have entered the earth if Adam and Eve had just obeyed God. But, of course, we all know what happened. Instead of subduing the devil, they listened to his lies and obeyed his command. As a result, they lost their authority in the earth, their right standing with God, and their garden home. Through this one act of disobedience to God's command, Adam and Eve paved the way for the curse to enter the earth.

But long before any sin was ever committed, God had a plan that would reverse the curse and restore mankind to right standing with Him. Before the foundation of the earth, it was settled in the throne room of Heaven that Jesus Christ would shed His blood to redeem mankind. This one act of love reversed the curse forever and shattered the power of the devil to steal, kill, and destroy God's creation. This one act of love also paved the way for God's blessing to be upon everyone that would believe His Word by faith.

From the beginning, blessing has been the central element of God's covenant with mankind. Think about the fact that the very first words Adam and Eve heard were blessing words. Even after the fall of Adam and Eve, God's covenant promise of *blessing* always reversed the curse on anyone that would obey Him by faith. In Genesis 12:3, God told Abraham, *"And I will bless them that bless thee, and curse him that curseth thee: and in thee shall all families of the earth be blessed."*

Pronouncing God's Blessing

Blessing is a powerful thing. Nelson's Illustrated Bible Dictionary defines it this way: "The act of declaring, or wishing, God's favor and goodness upon others. The blessing is not only the good effect of words; it also has the power to bring them to pass. In the Bible, important persons blessed those with less power or influence. The patriarchs pronounced benefits upon their children, often near their own deaths (Genesis 49:1-28). Even if spoken by mistake, once a blessing was given it could not be taken back (Genesis 27)."

Many years ago, when Jesse and I first understood this principle, we laid our hands on our daughter, Jodi, and pronounced God's blessing upon her life. We know from experience the value of saying blessing words over our family so that God can fulfill His covenant in the earth.

In Numbers, chapter six, God gave specific instructions about pronouncing His blessing on others:

> *And the LORD spake unto Moses, saying,*
>
> *Speak unto Aaron and unto his sons, saying, On this wise ye shall bless the children of Israel, saying unto them,*
>
> *The LORD bless thee, and keep thee:*
>
> *The LORD make His face shine upon thee, and be gracious unto thee:*
>
> *The LORD lift up His countenance upon thee, and give thee peace.*
>
> *And they shall put My name upon the children of Israel, and I will bless them.*
>
> NUMBERS 6:22-27

When we pronounce a blessing on someone, it is not a light thing; it is a strong thing. It is a command that is recognized in Heaven and changes people on Earth. Every time we say "God bless you," it should remind us that the curse has been reversed and the blessing has been restored.

Redeemed from the Curse

As born-again believers, we are not subject to the curse of the law. In Galatians 3:13-14, the Bible says, *"Christ hath redeemed us from the curse of the law, being made a curse for us: for it is written, Cursed is every one that hangeth on a tree: That **the blessing** of Abraham might come on the Gentiles through Jesus Christ; that we might receive the promise of the Spirit through faith."*

Jesus Christ, the Anointed One, has reversed the curse and paved the way to the blessing. His blood has redeemed you from any curse that would want to come across your path. If sickness or any curse listed in Deuteronomy 28:15-68 attacks your household, you can take authority over it. You don't have to put up with an attack from the devil!

No wonder the devil works overtime to stop you from studying the Bible or faithfully attending church. He knows that it's all over for him the moment you discover the authority given to you by Jesus Christ.

In Luke 10:19, Jesus declared, *"Behold, I give unto you power to tread on serpents and scorpions, and over all the power of the enemy: and nothing shall by any means hurt you."* And in John 14:14, He gave you authority to use His name: *"If ye shall ask any thing in My name, I will do it."*

That's exactly what happened in Acts 3:6 to the paralyzed man that sat at the gate of the city. When he asked for alms, Peter said, *"Silver and gold have I none; but such as I have give I thee: In the name of Jesus Christ of Nazareth rise up and walk."* The authority to use the name of Jesus instantly healed that man. He was so excited that he took off running and leaping and praising God.

When you have the authority to use someone's name, it is as though they were standing there in person. When you use the name of Jesus in faith, everything that is named has to bow. Actually, the devil messed up when he put a name on your problem. The Bible says in Philippians 2:10-11, *"That at the name of Jesus every knee should bow, of things in Heaven, and things in earth, and things under the earth; And that every tongue should confess that Jesus Christ is Lord, to the glory of God the Father."* So cancer has to bow, poverty has to bow, oppression has to bow, fear has to bow, and every name that is named has to bow!

In the book of Ephesians, Paul prayed this very powerful prayer that is now available to you through Christ Jesus:

> That the God of our Lord Jesus Christ, the Father of glory, may give unto you the spirit of wisdom and revelation in the knowledge of Him:

The eyes of your understanding being enlightened; that ye may know what is the hope of His calling, and what the riches of the glory of His inheritance in the saints,

And what is the exceeding greatness of His power to usward who believe, according to the working of His mighty power,

Which He wrought in Christ, when He raised Him from the dead, and set Him at His own right hand in the heavenly places,

Far above all principality, and power, and might, and dominion, and every name that is named, not only in this world, but also in that which is to come:

And hath put all things under His feet, and gave Him to be the head over all things to the church . . .

And hath raised us up together, and made us sit together in heavenly places in Christ Jesus.

EPHESIANS 1:17-22, 2:6

You are seated with Christ and blessed with full authority to use His name to bust the devil's head back into the dust. So get busy!

Protection from the Curse

Throughout the Bible we can read about people who were victorious when they believed God's Word and walked by faith. Just think about the curse, or plague, that came to destroy the firstborn of Egypt in Exodus, chapter 12.

God gave specific instructions to the Hebrews to apply the blood over their door posts so that the destroyer could not enter into their homes. Those that obeyed actually reversed the curse that was on that land. They were set apart for protection and salvation because of their obedience to the Word of God.

However, if they refused to obey God, all of the firstborn in their households would die along with those of the Egyptians. Now that would *not* have been God's fault. He clearly revealed to them how they would be protected from the curse that had come upon the land because of sin. It was up to them to do something about it. They had to walk in obedience and do what God had called them to do, and so will you.

"I Will Bless Them"

When God sent Jesus to the cross, He had *your* blessing on His mind. Ephesians 1:3 says, *"Blessed be the God and Father of our Lord Jesus Christ, Who **hath** blessed us with **all** spiritual blessings in heavenly places in Christ."* Everything we could possibly need to be an overcomer in this life is ours *in Christ!*

Take a moment and think of any spiritual blessing that comes to mind. You may even think of a few. Now, realize that God has already given it to you! You have a promise to be blessed in everything that you do (Deuteronomy 28:8). You have a promise to be empowered to prosper in every area of your life (3 John 2). You are redeemed from the curse of the law so that you can walk in boldness, wisdom, favor, strength, and have victory every single day of your life. Knowledge of this truth gives you power to run into the enemy's camp and take back all that has been stolen from you.

How do you do that? By boldly declaring God's promises and enforcing His will for your life. With your heart and mouth, you need to say things like: "The curse has been reversed. I am the blessed of the Lord. I am empowered to prosper in every area of my life. I am the head and not the tail. I am above and not beneath. I am walking in favor. I am walking in promise. My body is whole in the name of Jesus!"

Search out God's promises to you and *rehearse the verse!* Stand firm on God's covenant promises to you and declare: "I am redeemed from the curse of the law! I don't have to be sick. I don't have to be poor. I don't have to be oppressed. The blessings of Abraham are mine!"

Once you know who you are in Jesus, you realize that you are not walking around alone in this life. God Himself is dwelling *inside you,* empowering you to prosper. When you begin to take hold of how much God has already done for you, it is not only going to transform your life; it's also going to transform all those that are around you. Don't be surprised if you hear people start to say things like, "Who is this person?" "This is not the same person I grew up with." "You are changed!" "What is different about you?"

I believe that God wants to strengthen you today and let you know how much He loves you. He loves you so much that He sent Jesus to reverse the curse over your life and to bless you eternally in Heaven *and* in this present life on earth. Once you accept Jesus as your personal Savior, you are no longer under the curse of the law. Sin, sickness, and oppression of any kind have been eradicated by the blood of Jesus Christ.

The blessing God promised to Abraham's seed belongs to you and all that will obey His Word by faith. Receive God's blessing today!

CHAPTER 3

BANKRUPT the Devil!

God has given every born-again believer the authority to put the devil out of business on the earth. You could say we are on a divine assignment to bankrupt the devil. I believe that we need to serve notice on that loser that his days of stealing, killing, and destroying are over!

The truth is that the devil's power over mankind came to a screeching halt when Jesus sacrificed His life on the cross of Calvary. The Word of God declares that Jesus descended into the lower parts of the earth, set the captives free, and then ascended up far above all the heavens (Ephesians 4:8-10). And in Colossians 2:15, we learn that Jesus *"spoiled principalities and powers, He made a shew of them openly, triumphing over them in it."*

Jesus made a public exhibit of the devil in the court of Heaven, paid the penalty for the sins of the world, and redeemed mankind from the curse of the law with His own blood (Galatians 3:13-14, 29; Deuteronomy 28:15-68). As far as Heaven is concerned, the devil has been stripped of all power. Jesus solved the sin problem, failure problem, fear problem, depression problem, sickness problem, poverty problem, and every problem that will ever be named. Glory!

Our responsibility is to believe God's Word and take captive every thought that rises up against His promises to us. The Word of God tells us how:

> *For though we walk (live) in the flesh, we are not carrying on our warfare according to the flesh and using mere human weapons.*
>
> *For the weapons of our warfare are not physical [weapons of flesh and blood], but they are mighty before God for the overthrow and destruction of strongholds,*
>
> *[Inasmuch as we] refute arguments and theories and reasonings and every proud and lofty thing that sets itself up against the [true] knowledge of God; and we lead every thought and purpose away captive into the obedience of Christ, (the Messiah, the Anointed One).*
>
> 2 Corinthians 10:3-5 (AMPC)

As you can see, the weapons of our warfare are mighty through God. And, as a believer, you have the authority to use the name of Jesus to bind the devil from stealing what belongs to you. Faith in His Word will destroy every stronghold and overthrow the devil's arguments, theories, and reasonings that say, "Your family will never be saved," or "You'll never be used by God," or "Sickness runs in your family," or "No one cares about you," or "You'll never be debt free," or "You will never recover from this attack of the enemy."

Take a stand against thoughts of lack and failure by boldly declaring God's promises of abundance and victory. "I am of God and overcome all things by the blood of the Lamb and by the word of my testimony. Greater is He that is in me, than he that is in the world" (Revelation 12:11; 1 John 4:4). "Surely Jesus has borne my griefs, sorrows, and pain, and by His stripes I am healed" (Isaiah 53:4-5; 1 Peter 2:24). "I have given and it shall be given unto me; good measure, pressed down, shaken together, and running over, shall men give into my bosom. I submit to God and I resist the devil, therefore he will flee from me, in Jesus' name" (Luke 6:38; James 4:7). That's how you bankrupt the devil. Declaring God's Word strips the devil of every bit of power over your life. Glory to God!

When God began to talk to me about bankrupting the devil, He revealed three words: expose, destroy, and restore. You see, Jesus came to *expose* the thief, *destroy* the works of the thief, and *restore* everything the thief has stolen.

EXPOSE the Thief

I don't know about you, but I am fed up with people blaming God for what the devil has done. Jesus exposed the thief and set the record straight when He said in John 10:10 (AMPC), *"The thief comes only in order to steal and kill and destroy. I came that they may have and enjoy life, and have it in abundance (to the full, till it overflows)."* This verse makes it clear that Jesus came to give you an overflowing life. God has empowered you with dominion and authority to overcome any demonic force that comes to steal, kill, or destroy the successful life that He designed for you. He wants you to soar in this life.

At the time that Jesus announced this truth, the people had no revelation yet of the devil. They thought that both everything good and everything bad came from God. But when Jesus walked on the scene, He *exposed* the thief as the one that steals, kills, and destroys. The scriptures reveal that our God is good and His plans for us are good.

> *And the LORD thy God will bring thee into the land which thy fathers possessed, and thou shalt possess it; and He will do thee good, and multiply thee above thy fathers.*
> *And the LORD thy God will circumcise thine heart, and the heart of thy seed, to love the LORD thy God with all thine heart, and with all thy soul, that thou mayest live.*
> *And the LORD thy God will put all these curses upon thine enemies, and on them that hate thee, which persecuted thee.*
> *And thou shalt return and obey the voice of the LORD, and do all His commandments which I command thee this day.*
> *And the LORD thy God will make thee plenteous in every work of thine hand, in the fruit of thy body, and in the fruit of thy cattle, and in the fruit of thy land, for good: for the LORD will again rejoice over thee for good, as He rejoiced over thy fathers:*
> DEUTERONOMY 30:5-9

Once you settle the issue in your heart and mind that God wants you to succeed, it will free you to launch an attack on the devil and send him running. The question you may now have is, "How did the devil get to me?" Well, sometimes you open the door for the attack from the devil through ignorance or disobedience to God and His Word. However, I also know that sometimes the devil has gained access illegally and attacks without cause (Job 2:3). But regardless of how the attack came, the end result is still up to you. James 4:7

says, *"Submit yourselves therefore to God. Resist the devil, and he will flee from you."*

DESTROY the Works of the Thief

I want you to realize that Jesus came to destroy the works of the devil. That means that the devil can't even work—he is on disability! First John 3:8 says, *". . . For this purpose the Son of God was manifested, that He might destroy the works of the devil."* And Hebrews 2:14-15 says, *". . . that through death He might destroy him that had the power of death, that is, the devil; And deliver them who through fear of death were all their lifetime subject to bondage."*

Jesus disabled the devil and made him powerless to affect you. But for thousands of years, the devil has been taking drastic measures to avoid bankruptcy by having "going out of business" sales. As a result, the world has been flooded with false advertising that is specifically designed to trap unsuspecting customers into buying his bag of goods.

However, the devil's tactics are ineffective against those who know the Word of God and follow Jesus' example of walking with God. Acts 10:38 tells us, *"How God anointed Jesus of Nazareth with the Holy Ghost and with power: Who went about doing good, and healing all that were oppressed of the devil; for God was with Him."* So then, every believer has a responsibility to put the devil out of business in the same way that Jesus did—by doing good and healing all that are oppressed of the devil.

God's covenant promise to heal His children has always been available. Exodus 15:26 says, *"If thou wilt diligently hearken to the voice of the LORD thy God, and wilt do that which is right in His sight, and wilt give ear to His commandments, and keep all His statutes, I will put none of these diseases* upon thee, which I have brought upon the Egyptians: for I am the LORD that healeth thee."

That is why Jesus rebuked the religious leaders with these powerful words in Luke 13:16: *"And ought not this woman, being a daughter of Abraham, whom Satan hath bound, lo, these eighteen years, be loosed from this bond on the sabbath day?"* Just as Jesus expected the Jewish leaders of that day to destroy the works of the devil, He expects it of us, too.

Jesus said, *"And I will give unto thee the keys of the kingdom of Heaven: and whatsoever thou shalt bind on earth shall be bound in Heaven: and whatsoever thou shalt loose on earth shall be loosed in Heaven"* (Matthew 16:19). This makes it clear that we ought to be enforcing God's Word in the earth and loosing people from the bondage of the devil and destroying his works.

RESTORE Everything the Thief has Stolen

Isn't it time you took back everything that the devil has stolen from your life? Proverbs 6:31 declares that if the thief is found, *"he shall restore sevenfold; he shall give all the substance of his house."* I especially like the last part of that verse. I have served notice on the devil to turn over all the substance of his house.

According to the American Heritage Dictionary, the word *bankrupt* is defined as: "A debtor that, upon voluntary petition, or one invoked by the debtor's creditors is judged legally insolvent. The debtor's remaining property is then administered for the creditors or is distributed among them."

Everything that the devil has was stolen from God and His children. Jesus exposed the thief and destroyed his power to keep what rightfully belongs to you and me. That is why we can stand in full assurance and demand all the substance of his house. After all, Jesus has the keys to his front door (hell, Revelation 1:18) and his retirement home (bottomless pit, Revelation 20:1-3)!

God's promise of restoration of all things to His children must be fulfilled *before* He can send Jesus Christ back to the earth. This is clearly stated in Acts 3:20-21,25:

> *And He shall send Jesus Christ, which before was preached unto you:*
>
> *Whom the Heaven must receive until the times of restitution of all things, which God hath spoken by the mouth of all His holy prophets since the world began . . .*
>
> *Ye are the children of the prophets, and of the covenant which God made with our fathers, saying unto Abraham, And in thy seed shall all the kindreds of the earth be blessed.*

God is looking for people that will stand their ground, defy the lies of the devil, and boldly believe His promises. These are the last days, and we must declare that it is payday for the Body of Christ. It is time for you to get your stuff. It is time for you to bankrupt the devil!

CHAPTER 4

It's Time for You TO THRIVE

In life, seasons come and go. The Bible says there is *"A time to be born, and a time to die; a time to plant, and a time to pluck up that which is planted"* (Ecclesiastes 3:2). After many years of trying to grow beautiful and healthy houseplants, I have finally conceded that this is just not the season of my life for it. I seem to be continually living in the season to "pluck up that which is planted!" It's just not right.

Now I really do care about those plants, but the fact is that God has called me to the ministry and that means traveling. When I'm on the road with Jesse, we're seeing people's lives changed. They're getting saved, healed, and delivered. I don't even think about the plants until I arrive home from a ministry trip. I walk through my door, and there they are . . . begging for water and about ready to bite the dust. Every time I come home, it seems as if I am reviving them from yet another near-death experience.

Although my plants can miraculously survive weeks of neglect, they will never live up to their full potential this way. They will never thrive under this type of treatment. Even though I faithfully remove their dead leaves, add more fertilizer or replace potting soil again and again, I know that it's not right for my houseplants to keep existing in "survival mode." I want to do right by them. I want them to *thrive!*

God feels the same way about you. You don't need to spend your life on a treadmill, going through the motions and sweating up a storm but never going anywhere. God desires for you to *thrive* instead of continually living in survival mode. You were created in His image and given dominion over the works of God's hands. You were made more than a conqueror in this life by Jesus Christ. You are anointed to win and impossible to curse!

The definition of *thrive* is: "To make steady progress; prosper. To grow vigorously; flourish." That sounds like the very thing that God had in mind when He created Adam and Eve and placed them in a beautiful garden home. He told them to be fruitful and multiply—in other words, *thrive!* But they never did live up to their full potential. They never flourished. Although God had a plan for them to thrive, all they ever did was survive.

Their story is the oldest in the world, but we can still learn valuable lessons from Adam and Eve's failure. If we listen to God's Word and refuse to accept the lies of the devil, we can thrive. It is possible to "make steady progress, prosper, grow vigorously, and flourish" in any area of life. King David learned that lesson and, under the inspiration of the Holy Ghost, he wrote:

> *Blessed is the man that walketh not in the counsel of the ungodly, nor standeth in the way of sinners, nor sitteth in the seat of the scornful.*
>
> *But his delight is in the law of the LORD; and in His law doth he meditate day and night.*
>
> *And he shall be like a tree planted by the rivers of water, that bringeth forth his fruit in his season; his leaf also shall not wither; and whatsoever he doeth shall prosper.*
>
> PSALM 1:1-3

In the first three amazing verses of this Psalm, we can see God's three-step plan for us to thrive in whatever we do in life. If we 1.) choose not to hang with the wrong crowd and 2.) crave God's Word and feed on it, we shall 3.) live a fruitful, long, and prosperous life!

Don't Hang with the Wrong Crowd

That first word, *"Blessed,"* in verse one should really catch your attention. One definition of *blessed* is: "empowered to prosper." If you want to move out of survival mode and begin to thrive in life, you can gain tremendous insight from this verse.

The Amplified Bible, Classic Edition says, *"BLESSED (HAPPY, fortunate, prosperous, and enviable) is the man who walks and lives not in the counsel of the ungodly [following their advice, their plans and purposes], nor stands [submissive and inactive] in the path where sinners walk, nor sits down [to relax and rest] where the scornful [and the mockers] gather."*

This verse should be a warning flag. It is difficult to thrive when you are continually surrounded by ungodly sinners that mock God. It may be possible to survive in that environment, but you may never reach your greatest potential.

Hanging continually with the wrong crowd will stunt your growth and rob you of the power to succeed.

You may know people like those described above. They may even live in your house or work with you on the job. You are called to love them, pray for them, and lead them to Jesus, but they should not be influencing your daily life. Your blessed, thriving life should attract them to the Gospel. You are blessed and empowered to prosper by the Creator, God—anointed to win and impossible to curse! Your thriving, fruitful life and intimate relationship with God should be a beacon of light to the world, guiding them to safety.

One of the trademarks of a blessed person is the company they keep. A blessed person is attracted to those who are serious about their walk with God—they cultivate good relationships. A blessed person is a leader and not a follower—they don't follow the advice of the ungodly and don't make decisions that are influenced by ungodly plans and purposes. They don't choose the path of least resistance—they refuse to hang with those who are scornful of God's Word.

Proverbs 2:6-9 says:

> *For the LORD giveth wisdom: Out of His mouth cometh knowledge and understanding.*
>
> *He layeth up sound wisdom for the righteous: He is a buckler to them that walk uprightly.*
>
> *He keepeth the paths of judgment, and preserveth the way of His saints.*
>
> *Then shalt thou understand righteousness, and judgment, and equity; yea, every good path.*

God wants to reveal every good path to you. He has laid up sound wisdom that will enable you to live up to your full potential. Proverbs 3:5-6 reveals how you can find your pathway in life: *"Trust in the Lord with all thine heart; and lean not unto thine own understanding. In all thy ways acknowledge Him, and He shall direct thy paths."*

Crave God's Word and Feed on It

Let's look again at Psalm 1:2 (AMPC): *"But his delight and desire are in the law of the Lord, and on His law (the precepts, the instructions, the teachings of God) he habitually meditates (ponders and studies) by day and by night."*

A strong desire for God's Word is a dominate characteristic of the person that is blessed. Psalm 105:3-4 (AMPC) says, *"Glory in His holy name; let the hearts of those rejoice who seek and require the Lord [as their indispensable necessity]. Seek, inquire of and for the Lord, and crave Him and His strength (His might and inflexibility to temptation); seek and require His face and His presence [continually] evermore."* Once you taste and see that the Lord is good, you will forever crave Him and seek out ways to continually feed on His Word.

I'll never forget the look on my daughter's face when I fed her that first bite of "real food." Until that day, Jodi was content with strained carrots and bland rice cereal. She had no idea what she had been missing until I placed a spoonful of mashed potatoes and gravy in her mouth. Her beautiful blue eyes were so expressive as they locked on the dish in front of her. Before she could swallow her first bite, she grunted for more spoonfuls until it was all gone. After that day, Jodi wasn't satisfied with bland baby food. She had developed a craving for "real food" and refused to eat anything else.

In order to thrive in life, you need to understand the value of regularly feeding on the Word of God. A blessed person understands that regularly feeding on the Word of God is vital to their success in life. Craving God's Word, feeding on it regularly, and declaring it with your own mouth will empower you to thrive in life. Psalm 19:14 says, *"Let the words of my mouth, and the meditation of my heart, be acceptable in thy sight, O LORD, my Strength, and my Redeemer."*

Live a Fruitful, Long & Prosperous Life

If you refuse to hang with the wrong crowd and are determined to feed on God's Word, you can expect to thrive in life. Psalm 1:3 (AMPC) says, *"And he shall be like a tree firmly planted [and tended] by the streams of water, ready to bring forth its fruit in its season; its leaf also shall not fade or wither; and everything he does shall prosper [and come to maturity]."*

If you are planted firmly in God's Word and tended by His refreshing, living water, you are primed and ready to bring forth fruit. Instead of fading out or withering away, you have God's promise that everything you do will prosper. This is your season! You have moved out of survival mode and are on your way to thriving.

Today, I want to encourage you that your future is not bleak or weak, but strong and mighty. God's plan is for you to thrive, flourish, and live a fruitful life. You can be like those described in Psalm 92:12-14:

> *The righteous shall flourish like the palm tree: he shall grow like a cedar in Lebanon.*
> *Those that be planted in the house of the Lord shall flourish in the courts of our God.*
> *They shall still bring forth fruit in old age; they shall be fat and flourishing.*

Notice that this promise is for the righteous—that's you, if you have received Jesus as the Lord of your life. Regardless of your background or age, you can thrive and live a long, fruitful, and prosperous life. It may not come to you overnight, but if you plant yourself in the house of the Lord and are faithful to live by the Word, God has promised that you *"shall be fat and flourishing."* So don't let the little things steal God's good plan for your life. Decide today that you are going to do what it takes to thrive and be successful in every area of your life.

CHAPTER 5

Take the Path to THE GOOD LIFE

In South Louisiana, we have an abundance of seafood and, boy, do we know how it should be cooked! It's all about flavor and spice. One of my favorite local television commercials was from many years ago, and it began with a scene of an outdoor picnic table loaded with fresh, steaming seafood of every type you can imagine. The last time I saw the commercial, I could almost smell the seasoning through the television screen! Just as I began to lick my lips, the camera backed up slightly to reveal the back of a large man also looking at the tantalizing table loaded down with the good of our land. Just then, that man turned to look straight at me through steam-filled eyeglasses, and with a huge grin, declared, "Life is good!" Now even if you hate seafood, you know that man was talking about abundance.

Abundance has always been God's will for His children. To those who are willing and obedient, He promises that they will **eat the good** of the land (Isaiah 1:19). That is the quality of life that God offers to each of us today.

I believe that when God promised that we would eat the good of the land, He wasn't just talking about a full belly. He was talking about a full life—one that is filled with joy, peace, love, and every good thing that Heaven has to offer. We can *expect* a boundless supply of healing for the sick and salvation for the lost. We can *expect* deliverance for the captives and prosperity for the poor. This is the kind of abundant life that Jesus came to give you and me, and it is good! It's the life you were *created* to enjoy.

While most people will agree that God wants them to *be* a good person and *do* good works, many of those same people haven't realized that God also wants them to *live* the good life. The truth is that God has created all of us with that in mind.

> *For we are God's [own] handiwork (His workmanship), recreated in Christ Jesus, [born anew] that we may do those good works which God predestined (planned beforehand) for us [taking paths which He prepared ahead of time], that we should walk in them [**living the good life** which He prearranged and made ready for us to live].*
>
> EPHESIANS 2:10 (AMPC)

Isn't that amazing? God has good things that He has prearranged for you to walk in. If there seems to be a wall between you and the good life, settle the fact once and for all that God is not holding out on you. The problem is never with God. I have discovered three steps that have helped me to stay on the path to the good life. I hope they will help you, too.

Step One: Be Thankful

Being thankful is the first step in the path to the good life that God has for you. Although your life may be anything but good at this moment, you can be thankful that Jesus came to change all that. Psalm 100:4 in The Passion Translation says, *"You can pass through His open gates with the password of praise. Come right into His presence with thanksgiving. Come bring your thank offering to Him and affectionately bless His beautiful name!"*

Once you are thankful and acknowledge that He came to lead you out of a life of despair and into the good life, it won't be long before He will show you His path for your life. Proverbs 3:6 says, *"In all thy ways acknowledge Him, and He shall direct thy paths."*

God's Word can lead you out of lack and into abundance in every area of your life. Psalm 16:11 says, *"Thou wilt shew me the path of life: in Thy presence is fulness of joy; at Thy right hand there are pleasures for evermore."* Establish the fact in your heart that God is *always* looking to do you good.

Step Two: Walk Uprightly

This leads me to the second step in the path toward the good life, which is to walk uprightly. This simply means to walk in integrity and truth. When you are determined to always do what is right and always do it right, the byproduct of that is the good life.

Jesus said, *"But seek (aim at and strive after) first of all His kingdom and His righteousness (His way of doing and being right), and then all these things taken together will be given you besides"* (Matthew 6:33 AMPC).

When your life is focused on God's way of doing things and walking uprightly, Jesus promised that you would have all you need to eat, drink, and wear. However, having these life essentials is just the beginning of the good life that God has in mind for you. You can have hope for a successful life for yourself and your family. You were created by God, and through Christ Jesus you can live the good life. Although you may not be walking in every facet of it right now, it is available to *every* believer, including you.

Step Three: Sow Your Seed

The third step on the path that will lead you into this good life must begin with a seed offering. Once your heart has been changed and things do not control you, you will need to recognize that God's plan to move you out of lack will always begin by giving to God.

It is vitally important that we are obedient when God reveals what we are to do with the seed that He gives to us. We bind His ability to meet our needs when we do not yield to the spirit of giving. The principles that God established in His Word will guide us through the desert and bring us to the land of milk and honey. We serve a God that specializes in making a way where there is no way.

Second Corinthians 9:10-11 (AMPC) says: *"And [God] Who provides seed for the sower and bread for eating will also provide and multiply your [resources for] sowing and increase the fruits of your righteousness [which manifests itself in active goodness, kindness and charity]. Thus you will be enriched in all things and in every way, so that you can be generous, and [your generosity as it is] administered by us will bring forth thanksgiving to God."*

If you want to reap, you must sow. And like we just read, the good news is that God will provide seed to the sower. Once you thankfully offer back to God what is rightfully His, you are actually investing in your own prosperity. God is able to put His kingdom principle of sowing *and* reaping to work for you. Your obedience will result in blessing. Paul made this truth clear to the Galatians when he said:

> *Let him that is taught in the word communicate unto him that teacheth in all **good things.***
>
> *Be not deceived; God is not mocked: for whatsoever a man soweth, that shall he also reap.*
>
> *For he that soweth to his flesh shall of the flesh reap corruption; but he that soweth to the Spirit shall of the Spirit reap life everlasting.*
>
> *And let us not be weary in well doing: for in due season we shall reap, if we faint not.*
>
> *As we have therefore opportunity, let us **do good** unto all men, especially unto them who are of the household of faith.*
>
> GALATIANS 6:6-10

That word *communicate* translates "contribute" in the Amplified Bible versions. Paul was teaching them the principle that reaping is always the result of sowing into good soil. This truth is reinforced in the book of Philippians, which says:

> *Always in every prayer of mine for you all making request with joy,*
>
> *For your **fellowship** in the Gospel from the first day until now;*
>
> *Being confident of this very thing, that He which hath begun a **good work** in you will perform it until the day of Jesus Christ.*
>
> PHILIPPIANS 1:4-6

The people in the church at Philippi were faithful Partners to the apostle Paul. The Amplified Bible, Classic Edition translates the word *fellowship* in verse five to mean *"(your sympathetic cooperation and contributions and partnership)."* They had been instrumental in advancing the Gospel, and Paul wanted them to know that they were destined for good fruit to abound to their heavenly account. They could expect God to supply all of their needs. Later in this same book, Paul told the Philippians:

> Now ye Philippians know also, that in the beginning of the Gospel, when I departed from Macedonia, no church **communicated** with me as concerning **giving and receiving**, but ye only.
>
> For even in Thessalonica ye sent once and again unto my necessity.
>
> Not because I desire a gift: but I desire fruit that may abound to your account.
>
> But I have all, and abound: I am full, having received of Epaphroditus the things which were sent from you, an odour of a sweet smell, a sacrifice acceptable, wellpleasing to God.
>
> But my **God shall supply all your need** according to His riches in glory by Christ Jesus.
>
> PHILIPPIANS 4:15-19

Paul knew the principle: If you give, you shall receive. God's way of supplying all your need was revealed by Jesus in Luke 6:38. There, He promised: *"Give, and it shall be given unto you; good measure, pressed down, and shaken together, and running over, shall men give into your bosom. For with the same measure that ye mete withal it shall be measured to you again."* It is Christ's desire to give you a life that is so full, it is literally running over and spilling onto others.

God sent His Son, Jesus, to bring this message to the world. In fact, in His first sermon, Jesus boldly preached about *"the accepted and acceptable year of the Lord [the day when salvation and the free favors of God profusely abound]"* (Luke 4:19 AMPC).

We know that God's Word cannot change, and it will not return to Him void. It will accomplish that which He sent it to do. God *will* have a generation that will receive His promise and welcome this day *"when salvation and the free favors of God profusely abound."*

That word *profusely* means "to radiate with abundance; plentifully, abundantly, extravagantly, freely." Now that ought to make you shout! Those are the kind of *"free favors"* our God has prepared for His children—and it is this kind of blessed life that you were created to live! This is not just a suggestion from your Creator; it is His command, which you'll see in the following passage:

> *If you will listen diligently to the voice of the Lord your God, being watchful to do all His commandments which I command you this day, the Lord your God will set you high above all the nations of the earth.*
>
> *And all these blessings shall come upon you and overtake you if you heed the voice of the Lord your God.*
>
> *Blessed shall you be in the city and blessed shall you be in the field.*
>
> *Blessed shall be the fruit of your body and the fruit of your ground and the fruit of your beasts, the increase of your cattle and the young of your flock.*
>
> *Blessed shall be your basket and your kneading trough.*
>
> *Blessed shall you be when you come in and blessed shall you be when you go out.*

The Lord shall cause your enemies who rise up against you to be defeated before your face; they shall come out against you one way and flee before you seven ways.

The Lord shall command the blessing upon you in your storehouse and in all that you undertake. And He will bless you in the land which the Lord your God gives you.

The Lord will establish you as a people holy to Himself, as He has sworn to you, if you keep the commandments of the Lord your God and walk in His ways.

And all people of the earth shall see that you are called by the name [and in the presence of] the Lord, and they shall be afraid of you.

And the Lord shall make you have a surplus of prosperity, through the fruit of your body, of your livestock, and of your ground, in the land which the Lord swore to your fathers to give you.

The Lord shall open to you His good treasury, the heavens, to give the rain of your land in its season and to bless all the work of your hands; and you shall lend to many nations, but you shall not borrow.

And the Lord shall make you the head, and not the tail; and you shall be above only, and you shall not be beneath, if you heed the commandments of the Lord your God which I command you this day and are watchful to do them.

DEUTERONOMY 28:1-13 (AMPC)

Realize today that God has empowered *you* to prosper spiritually, physically, and financially. He wants you to be the head and not the tail, above and not beneath. You were created to be blessed coming in and blessed going out. You are the blessed of the Lord. Take the path to the good life and experience success today.

CHAPTER 6

Empowered
TO PROSPER

I once spoke to a Seminary graduate who, at that time, had recently discovered God's promises for prosperity. She was surprised that she didn't notice them before because she was suddenly finding scriptures about prosperity throughout the Bible. It was as though she discovered a precious map to a long-lost treasure chest. When I began to tell her about a new verse that I'd just found, her face lit up with excitement. As she walked away, I knew that she was on the right track. She was destined for success.

I guess I'm still shocked by the number of Christians that haven't discovered the truth about prosperity. You would think that the very first words that God spoke to mankind would settle that issue once and for all. The Bible records them in

Genesis 1:28: *"And God blessed them...."* That word *blessed* means *"empowered to prosper."*

Just those four little words would have been enough, but God did not stop there. The verse goes on to say, *"... and God said unto them, **Be fruitful**, and **multiply**, and **replenish** the earth, and **subdue** it: and have **dominion** over the fish of the sea, and over the fowl of the air, and over every living thing that moveth upon the earth."*

God's Will & God's Plan

Although you need to know that prosperity is God's *will*, you must also know God's *plan* to bring it to pass in your life. When you spend time in God's presence and in His Word, He will reveal His plans for your success.

You see, Moses knew that it was the *will* of God for the children of Israel to be delivered from slavery, but he didn't have a clue about God's *plan* to bring it to pass. Moses reacted in the flesh when he murdered the Egyptian and hid him in the sand. Years later, after seeking God's face and spending time in His presence, God's great plan was revealed and an entire nation of people was led out of bondage toward their Promised Land—toward a land that flowed with milk and honey. It was part of the divine plan for supernatural success for the children of God.

In the book of Numbers, chapters 13 and 14, we find the perfect example of a people that knew God's will but failed to walk in His plan. The children of Israel had been given specific instructions from God to spy out the land. Each of the twelve spies that were chosen represented their entire tribe and were told to *"... be ye of good courage, and bring of the fruit of the land ..."* (Numbers 13:20).

The children of Israel had heard about the Promised Land all of their lives. They had been told how *". . . the Lord made a covenant with Abram, saying, Unto thy seed have I given this land. . . "* (Genesis 15:18). Then they heard about God's words spoken to Moses from the burning bush: *"I am come down to deliver them out of the hand of the Egyptians, and to bring them up . . . unto a land flowing with milk and honey . . ."* (Exodus 3:8).

Now, when the twelve spies returned from their mission, they presented proof of the abundant, boundless supply that was in the land that God had promised them. But ten of the spies came back with an evil, unbelieving report and sent the entire nation into a tailspin. The Bible says in Numbers 14:1, *"And **all** the congregation lifted up their voice, and cried; and the people wept that night."* Why? Because they chose to believe the word of men instead of the Word of God. They rejected God's will and plan for their lives and began making their own plan to return to the bondage of Egypt.

But two of the spies, Joshua and Caleb, returned with a good report. They stood up for God and declared to the nation: *"If the Lord delight in us, then He will bring us into this land, and give it us; a land which floweth with milk and honey"* (Numbers 14:8).

Those two had discovered the key to success: *"If the Lord delight in us."* Well, how does the Lord delight in us? When we live by faith! Hebrews 11:6 says, **"But without faith it is impossible to please Him:** *for he that cometh to God must believe that He is, and that He is a rewarder of them that diligently seek Him."*

God has a plan to reward those that He delights in. Ecclesiastes 2:26 tells us, **"For God giveth to a man that is good** *in His sight wisdom, and knowledge, and joy: but to the sinner He giveth travail, to gather and to heap up,* **that He may give to him that is good before God."** And in Proverbs 13:22, it says, "A good man leaveth an inheritance to his children's children: and **the wealth of the sinner is laid up for the just.**"

The only way you can be *good* or *just* before God is by faith. The Bible declares four different times that "the just" are those that "live by faith." My favorite is found in Hebrews 10:38: *"Now the just shall live by faith: but if any man draw back, My soul shall have no pleasure in him."*

Joshua and Caleb knew that there was serious wealth in the land of milk and honey that was laid up for those that God delighted in. In Numbers 14:9, they warned the people:

> *Only rebel not ye against the LORD, neither fear ye the people of the land; for they are bread for us: their defence is departed from them, and the LORD is with us: fear them not.*

Now we know from verse 10 that the people not only rejected the wisdom of Joshua and Caleb, but they also demanded that Moses and Aaron be stoned to death. But before the first stone was hurled, the glory of the Lord appeared at the Tent of Meeting before all the Israelites. God said to Moses in verse 11, *"How long will this people provoke Me? And how long will it be ere they believe Me?"*

Today, you and I face a similar challenge: How long will it be before we decide to believe God's promise for an abundant, boundless supply? Since the day God created mankind and spoke the first words of blessing, He had a plan of success for His creation. I believe that God is looking for a generation of people that will believe Him and walk in divine prosperity.

In studying this story and the strong warning in Numbers 14:9, I saw four things the children of Israel had to do in order to walk out of lack and into the land of milk and honey. They had to be obedient to God, get rid of fear, know the limitations of their enemy, and know the power of their God. Those same four things will empower you to prosper and lead you into your land of success today.

Determine to be Obedient to God

The first part of Joshua and Caleb's warning in Numbers 14:9 says, *"Only rebel not ye against the LORD . . . ."* Regardless of any evil report you may hear, stick with God's Word and you can receive healing, favor, power, and anything you need.

Get Rid of Fear

The second part of the warning in Numbers 14:9 says, *". . . neither fear ye the people of the land . . . ."* I have heard fear defined as "faith in reverse." Fear is one of the main tools the devil uses to keep God's people from experiencing success in their lives.

The ten spies were infected with fear and it spread like wildfire through the entire congregation of Israel. They quickly forgot the power of God that had supernaturally delivered them from Egypt, the most powerful nation in the world. They yielded to fear and lost out on God's promise for their lives.

You don't have to yield to fear. If the infection of fear tries to set in, rebuke it in Jesus' name and boldly declare your promise in 2 Timothy 1:7: *"For God hath not given us the spirit of fear; but of power, and of love, and of a sound mind."*

Know the Limitations of Your Enemy

The third part of the warning dealt with exposing the limitations of your enemy. As you read in Numbers 13 and 14, you'll see how the ten spies came back from their trip whining about giants and a land that eats up its inhabitants. Today, the devil says it a little differently: "Are you crazy? If you try that, they will eat you up and spit you out."

But Joshua and Caleb saw it another way. They saw the giants and everything in that land as their God-ordained harvest and they were determined to go after it. They declared, *". . . for they are bread for us: their defence is departed from them. . . ."*

The Bible tells us that the reason Jesus came to the earth was so that He could destroy the works of the devil (1 John 3:8). No matter what lie the devil has been telling you today, 1 John 4:4 declares, *"Ye are of God, little children, and have overcome them: because greater is He that is in you, than he that is in the world."* The devil and his crowd are defenseless against a blood-bought child of God.

Know the Power of Your God

The fourth thing that I saw in Numbers 14:9 was the phrase *"the LORD is with us."* It wasn't enough for them to know that the defense of their enemy was departed; the children of Israel had to know that **God** was with them. The God that opened up the Red Sea so they could walk into the land of milk and honey was *with them.*

Joshua and Caleb knew the power of their God. And because of this, they were walking in the manifestation of Deuteronomy 8:18, which declares, *"But thou shalt remember the LORD thy God: for it is He that giveth thee power to get wealth, that He may establish His covenant which He sware unto thy fathers, as it is this day."*

It doesn't matter how big the enemy is or how impossible things look, once you know that God is *with you,* it changes everything. He has given you power to get wealth, walk in divine prosperity, and succeed in life. You can expect a harvest on every faith-filled seed that you sow. It is a vital part of His covenant promise to His children, and it will come to pass!

CHAPTER 7

GOD'S Reward System

Have you noticed that every God idea is a good idea? Our Heavenly Father's idea to send Jesus to be born of a virgin and die on the cross for the sins of the world has transported countless people out of the power of darkness and into His glorious light. Jesus taught us in John 3:16, *"For God so loved the world, that He gave His only begotten Son, that whosoever believeth in Him should not perish, but have everlasting life."* That one good idea from God has established an eternal reward for whosoever believes in Jesus.

Throughout the Word we see a God that rewards obedience, faithfulness, and faith. In fact, the very first time the Bible mentions the word *reward* is when God described Himself to Abram. Genesis 15:1 says, *"After these things the word of the*

Lord came unto Abram in a vision, saying, Fear not, Abram: I am thy Shield, and thy exceeding great reward."

When I studied the events that occurred before Abram received this vision, I discovered that he had just returned from battle to rescue his nephew, Lot, from prison. Along with Lot, Abram also brought back all the women, all of Lot's goods, and all of the goods of Sodom and Gomorrah that had been taken away. Then, after hearing about Abram's victory, Melchizedek (the King of Salem and priest) blessed him and said, *". . . Blessed be Abram of the Most High God, possessor of Heaven and earth: And blessed be the Most High God, which hath delivered thine enemies into thy hand. And he gave him tithes of all"* (Genesis 14:19-20).

Now the King of Sodom was very impressed with old Abram and wanted to reward him for returning his stuff. But Abram refused and told him, *"I have lift up mine hand unto the Lord, the Most High God, the possessor of Heaven and earth, that I will not take from a thread even to a shoelatchet, and that I will not take any thing that is thine, lest thou shouldest say, I have made Abram rich"* (Genesis 14:22-23).

You see, Abram was a man of principle who was totally committed to God's plan for his life. At seventy-five years old, he left his country and kindred in obedience to God because *"he looked for a city which hath foundations, whose builder and maker is God"* (Hebrews 11:10). He had the blessing of the Most High on his life, and according to Genesis 13:2, Abram was already very rich in cattle, silver, and gold. He wasn't looking for rewards from the King of Sodom. It was at this moment that God revealed Himself to Abram as his Shield and his *exceeding great reward.*

The Hebrew word for *reward* is defined as "payment of contract, wages, salary, or compensation." God is looking for ways to reward and bless all those who walk in obedience to His Word. Psalm 84:11 declares, *"For the LORD God is a Sun and Shield: the LORD will give grace and glory: no good thing will He withhold from them that walk uprightly."* And Psalm 31:23 says, *"O love the LORD, all ye His saints: for the LORD preserveth the faithful, and plentifully rewardeth the proud doer."*

Reward: The Result of Obedience

Jesse and I discovered early on the value of using a reward system with our daughter Jodi. She did not always understand or agree with our ideas, but she learned the system early in life. Her first steps were made reaching for a toy that she wanted, which I held just a step out of her reach. When she took the step toward it on her own, I let her have the toy. Soon, she was walking across the room carrying her toy.

When Jodi was in High School, we applied the same system and faithfully rewarded obedience. Jesse used to tell her, "Jodi, always obey your Mom and Dad and you will be blessed in the city and blessed in the mall. Blessed will you be in your car because your gas tank will be full. But if you disobey us, you will have to push your car to the mall." We weren't looking for ways to punish; we were looking for ways to bless!

Many parents motivate their children with rewards. I am sure you've heard this one: "If you clean your room, you can play outside." Another common motivation parents use is, "If you do your homework, you can watch TV." But my all-time favorite is, "If you eat all your dinner, you can have dessert!" Now that's a reward!

Several years ago, I decided it was time for a reward day for Jesse and Cathy Duplantis. Both of us had been dieting pretty strong, eating all the right foods and totally staying away from sugar. Our travel schedule had been hectic and we were at home enjoying a relaxing moment in front of the television. Just then, a commercial interrupted the old movie we were watching and I was inspired.

Now just the fact that we were actually watching an entire commercial was an odd thing. Jesse is lightning-fast with the remote control and always scans the channels during the commercial breaks looking for news, weather, or lions eating warthogs. But this time he was instantly captured by a vision of a piece of chocolate cake that was so fresh and moist that it bounced back with a fork. Both of us seemed to be frozen in time as we longingly watched the man put a forkful of that cake into his mouth. Jesse and I licked our lips, looked each other in the eye, and I said, "Would you like a cake, Honey?"

As soon as he nodded yes, I forgot about the movie and took off speeding down the street toward the store. I was on a mission: It was time for a reward! And in less than an hour after watching that commercial, our home was filled with the most wonderful sugary smell, and I was smoothing chocolate icing on our very own freshly baked yellow cake. Can you say "Mmmmmm"?

Now Jesse can mutilate a cake worse than anyone I know. He has a bad habit of putting his fork right into the cake for a mouthful. As you can imagine, I usually fuss and give him a hard time about it. But while the cake was in the oven, I thought of a way to let Jesse have his cake and eat it, too—and without any hassles from me.

After smoothing the icing on top of the double layer cake, I cut it right down the middle and told Jesse that one half was for him and the other was for me. Now my intent at the time was to just let him mutilate his half so that I could keep the other side nice and neat on the cake plate to serve to any guests that may decide to stop by our house. But that is not what happened at all. We were so hyped up for this cake, we each took our half and devoured it while it was still hot. It was our reward day and we enjoyed every gluttonous bite. Afterward, we looked guiltily at each other and Jesse jokingly said, "Cathy, we have sinned!" It was a long time before we allowed ourselves to have another chocolate cake reward day.

Rewards: Today and Eternally

Every person that accepts Jesus Christ as their Savior has God's promise of a life in Heaven as their eternal reward. Although this God idea has taken care of the sweet by-and-by, He also has awesome ideas to help you in the nasty here and now. Here are a few for you to study:

> Deuteronomy 30:19 – *"I call Heaven and earth to record this day against you, that I have set before you life and death, blessing and cursing: therefore choose life, that both thou and thy seed may live."*
>
> Psalm 68:19 – *"Blessed be the Lord, Who daily loadeth us with benefits, even the God of our salvation. Selah."*
>
> Jeremiah 29:11-14 (NASB) – *"'For I know the plans that I have for you,' declares the LORD, 'plans for welfare and not for calamity to give you a future and a hope. Then you will call upon Me and come and pray to Me, and I will listen to you. You will seek Me and find Me when you search for Me with all your heart. I will be found by you,' declares the LORD, 'and I will restore your fortunes and will gather you from all the nations and from all the places where I have driven you,' declares the LORD, 'and I will bring you back to the place from where I sent you into exile.'"*

I believe that God desires for each of us to have a greater appreciation and expectancy for His rewards—both eternally and today. Gone are the days of limitations. We have come too far to go back into lack. Jesus came to reveal His Father's plan to reward those who believe in Him with a successful life, overflowing with God's best.

This is not the time to be weary in well-doing, passed out on the floor as due season approaches. Hebrews 10:35-36 says, *"Cast not away therefore your confidence, which hath great recompense of reward. For ye have need of patience, that, after ye have done the will of God, ye might receive the promise."* God's promises of salvation, healing, deliverance, favor, wisdom, and peace are available to you today. They are all part of God's good plan to reward you.

CHAPTER 8

Destined for SUCCESS

A king that ruled in the days of Elisha was fascinated by the miraculous. He asked Gehazi, the servant of Elisha, *"Tell me some stories about the great things Elisha has done"* (2 Kings 8:4 NLT).

Gehazi had seen Elisha heal the leper Naaman and multiply a desperate widow's jar of oil until it was enough to pay off all of her bills and retire for life. But just as he was telling the king about Elisha's greatest miracle of restoring a dead boy to life, something unexpected happened. At that very moment, a woman had entered the throne room and was demanding the attention of the king.

Now this was unheard of in those days. You couldn't just walk into the presence of a king and start shouting your petition. Remember the story of Esther? She wanted to speak to the king, her husband, but she had to wait for him to speak first. If Esther dared to approach the throne without an invitation, she could have been killed.

Gehazi was very familiar with this woman from Shunem, who had just returned after being gone during the seven-year famine prophesied by Elisha, his former master. And it was not an accident that God had led this amazing woman to that very place and at that very moment. Let's read this amazing account:

> Elisha had told the woman whose son he had brought back to life, 'Take your family and move to some other place, for the Lord has called for a famine on Israel that will last for seven years.'
>
> So the woman **did as the man of God instructed.** She took her family and settled in the land of the Philistines for seven years.
>
> After the famine ended she returned from the land of the Philistines, and she went to see the king about getting back her house and land.
>
> As she came in, the king was talking with Gehazi, the servant of the man of God. The king had just said, 'Tell me some stories about the great things Elisha has done.'
>
> And Gehazi was telling the king about the time Elisha had brought a boy back to life. **At that very moment,** the mother of the boy walked in to make her appeal to the king about her house and land. 'Look, my lord the king!' Gehazi exclaimed. 'Here is the woman now, and this is her son—the very one Elisha brought back to life!'
>
> 'Is this true?' the king asked her. And she told him the story. So he directed one of his officials to see that **everything she had lost was restored to her,** including the value of any crops that had been harvested during her absence.
>
> 2 Kings 8:1-6 (NLT)

Why did the king grant that Shunammite woman's petition for her house and land, *and* grant her the value of seven years of harvest that would have been reaped from her land? After all, she did not even work for that harvest. It's because she was destined for success!

The Perceptive Are Destined for Success

In 2 Kings, chapter four, we learn of Elisha's first encounter with this woman:

> *One day Elisha went to the town of Shunem. A wealthy woman lived there, and she urged him to come to her home for a meal. After that, whenever he passed that way, he would stop there for something to eat.*
>
> *She said to her husband, 'I am sure this man who stops in from time to time is a holy man of God.*
>
> *Let's build a small room for him on the roof and furnish it with a bed, a table, a chair, and a lamp. Then he will have a place to stay whenever he comes by.'*
>
> *One day Elisha returned to Shunem, and he went up to this upper room to rest.*
>
> *He said to his servant Gehazi, 'Tell the woman from Shunem I want to speak to her.' When she appeared,*
>
> *Elisha said to Gehazi, 'Tell her, 'We appreciate the kind concern you have shown us. What can we do for you? Can we put in a good word for you to the king or to the commander of the army?"*
>
> *'No,' she replied, 'my family takes good care of me.'*
>
> 2 KINGS 4:8-13 (NLT)

From the moment that the Shunammite woman saw Elisha, she was sure he was a holy man of God. The King James

Version of 2 Kings 4:9 says, *"I perceive that this is an holy man of God, which passeth by us continually."*

Now, when you are obedient to the leading of the Spirit of God and partner up with a ministry, it is not a one-sided thing. You are laying the foundation to walk in the same power, favor, and anointing because you have literally become a part of that ministry.

By being sensitive to the needs of Elisha, the Shunammite woman was really honoring the God Who anointed him. According to Proverbs 3:9-10 (NLT), she was destined for success: *"Honor the LORD with your wealth and with the best part of everything you produce. Then He will fill your barns with grain, and your vats will overflow with good wine."* Success is the byproduct of honoring God and giving your firstfruits to Him. You can count on it!

So this was no ordinary woman that boldly entered the throne room with her son at the precise moment Gehazi and the king were discussing Elisha's greatest miracle. She was a faithful partner to the ministry of Elisha and determinedly saw to it that his needs were met. If he needed food, she fed him. If he needed a place to sleep, she made sure that he got it. Whatever God laid upon her heart to do for Elisha, that is exactly what she did.

That is exactly why God paved the Shunammite woman's way with divine favor that day with the king and had arranged every detail of her restoration. God is faithful and will not be mocked. He has promised in His Word that if you sow, you can expect to reap (Galatians 6:7). She had sown into the ministry of Elisha to provide for him, and she reaped her home, land, and the value of seven years of harvest on that land. Because she had been a faithful partner, she was supernaturally positioned for success and received an overflow harvest on the seeds she had obediently sown into that ministry.

The Prudent Are Destined for Success

We don't know much about her husband, but this Shunammite woman definitely had her stuff together. She was like the wife described in Proverbs 19:14 (AMPC), *"House and riches are the inheritance from fathers, but a wise, understanding, and prudent wife is from the Lord."*

The Nelson's Bible Dictionary defines *prudent* as "skill, good judgment, and common sense." Both King David and King Solomon were described in the Bible as men that were prudent and wise, and they were greatly used by God.

It is common sense to seek God and find ways to serve Him. Think about it: the Creator gives you opportunities to bless Him by ministering unto others. Why? He could just speak and new things, whatever is necessary, would suddenly come into existence. He could if He wanted to because He's God! But His plan is for you to serve Him from your heart and give in faith so that He has an opening to bring overflow and success into your life.

The Persistent Are Destined for Success

God's methods always work when you are persistent to obey His Word. A never-give-up attitude will enable you to stay focused on God's promise until you see it fulfilled. Some people never see their victory because they gave up just moments before it is manifested. But that doesn't have to be you! All you have to do is refuse to get weary in well-doing and faint not (Galatians 6:9). The persistent are destined for success!

The Shunammite woman was very persistent when it came to blessing the work of God. She didn't just invite Elisha to stop and eat bread, verse 8 in the King James Version of the Bible says she *constrained* him. That means she *laid hold of him* and insisted that he allow her to bless him. Not only did she feed him every chance that she got, but she also talked her husband into building an extra room on the house to make him comfortable while traveling through their town.

I believe that God moved upon this woman's heart in order to meet the needs of His servant, Elisha. He was so overwhelmed by her generosity, Elisha tells her, *"Behold, thou hast been careful for us with all this care; what is to be done for thee?"* (2 Kings 4:13).

You see, the Shunammite woman's perception, prudence, and persistence supernaturally positioned her for success. She was rewarded by God on the day that she stood before the king and received more than she could ask or think.

The principle is clear: When you do something for God, you will always be rewarded. She was not the first person to realize that you can't out-give God. He will not be a debtor to anyone. He will always send supernatural increase to those that sow in faith.

Our God has a boundless supply of everything you could ever need in this life and wants to position you for success. When you honor Him with your income and walk uprightly before Him, nothing can be withheld from you. One day God may ask you the same question that Elisha asked his faithful partner: *"What is to be done for thee?"*

CHAPTER 9

Turn Your Nothing into SOMETHING

Throughout the Bible, we are told about a God that specializes in doing the impossible. By faith He created the world out of nothing, hung it on nothing, and it became something. When the children of Israel were in the wilderness and had nothing to eat, He gave them something—manna from Heaven. During a great drought, God sent ravens to feed the prophet Elijah and turned his nothing into something. And when a destitute widow had nothing but a little pot of oil, God supernaturally turned her nothing into something. Now that is power!

Just like that widow woman with nothing but a pot of oil, you may think that your situation is hopeless and that nothing can get you out of the mess that you are in. But God is not limited to natural ways to meet your need. He moves in a much higher realm. He looks for opportunities to help you turn your nothing into something.

Stop Looking at Nothing—*Do* Something!

Time after time, the disciples saw Jesus do the miraculous. He overcame every situation, including a cruel death on the cross of Calvary. On two different occasions, the disciples saw Jesus feed multitudes with a few small fish and loaves of bread. Yet, when they were hungry and had one loaf to split between only twelve of them, they failed to do something about it. They focused on their lack of bread and did not remember the power of God that was available to them to multiply the bread. Jesus wanted them to learn how to turn their nothing into an abundant supply. Let's read the story in Mark, chapter eight:

> *Now the disciples had forgotten to take bread, neither had they in the ship with them more than one loaf.*
>
> *And He charged them, saying, Take heed, beware of the leaven of the Pharisees, and of the leaven of Herod.*
>
> *And they reasoned among themselves, saying, It is because we have no bread.*
>
> *And when Jesus knew it, He saith unto them, Why reason ye, because ye have no bread? perceive ye not yet, neither understand? have ye your heart yet hardened?*
>
> *Having eyes, see ye not? and having ears, hear ye not? and do ye not remember?*
>
> *When I brake the five loaves among five thousand, how many baskets full of fragments took ye up? They say unto Him, Twelve.*
>
> *And when the seven among four thousand, how many baskets full of fragments took ye up? And they said, Seven.*

And He said unto them, How is it that ye do not understand?
MARK 8:14-21

Many people see what they have as nothing and decide to give up and do nothing. The road to success is dotted with many tempting parking places, but God wants us to understand His principles and begin to DO something! The secret of success is to be like a duck: smooth and unruffled on top, but paddling furiously underneath.

You may be asking, "What can I do?" Many times, God's answer to you will be a question back to you: "What do you have?"

When your situation looks hopeless, you don't have to stand around and do nothing. God can use whatever is in your hand. You may think your hands are empty, but they are not. Your hands can always pray, praise, sow, and serve.

By an act of your will, you can change your defeat into victory. You can decide to obediently follow the leading of the Spirit of God and do what is in your hand to do. You see, faith *without* works is nothing, but faith *with* works is something (James 2:20,26).

There are three kinds of people in the world: the Wills, the Won'ts, and the Can'ts. The Wills accomplish everything, the Won'ts oppose everything, and the Can'ts fail in everything. But you don't have to lose at the game of life. You can become a winner!

A winner says, "Let's find out." A loser says, "Nobody knows." When a winner makes a mistake, he says, "I was wrong." When a loser makes a mistake, he says, "It wasn't my fault." A winner goes through a problem; a loser goes around it and never gets past it. A winner makes commitments; a loser makes promises. A winner says, "I'm good, but not as good as I ought to be." A loser says, "I'm not as bad as a lot of other people are." A winner tries to learn from those who are superior to him. A loser tries to tear down those who are superior to him. A winner says, "There ought to be a better way to do it." A loser says, "That's the way it's always been done here."

I once heard the story about a congregation that met to pray for rain to release a long dry spell. The preacher looked severely at his flock and said, "Brothers and Sisters, y'all know why we are here. Now, what I want to know is, where are your umbrellas?"

Real Bible faith sees the invisible, believes the incredible, and receives the impossible. When you sow, expect a harvest every time. When you pray, expect results every time. Don't just tell others about the labor pains you are going through, show them the baby. Don't stop believing until you deliver! Remember, God always has a plan to help you turn your nothing into something.

CHAPTER 10

God Wants You TO SUCCEED

Jesus is never limited to natural methods when it comes to providing for the needs of God's people. He never freaked out when multitudes of people stopped by unexpectedly for lunch. He didn't get discouraged if the fishing business was bad or if taxes had to be paid. Jesus knew that each situation He encountered was just another opportunity for God to be glorified.

The Bible says that Jesus went about doing good and healing all that were oppressed of the devil for God was with Him. Blinded eyes had to see, lame legs had to walk, and deaf ears had to hear because God had anointed Him with the Holy Ghost and power. Jesus was never overwhelmed by circumstances and He was never affected by public opinion. He wanted the world to experience the abundant life of success that knowing God could bring.

God's Plan for You: Multiply and Increase

God has always had a plan to bless and prosper His creation. As I have already mentioned, Adam and Eve were told to be fruitful and multiply. Abraham was promised a great increase that was compared to the stars in the heavens. *"And He brought him forth abroad, and said, Look now toward Heaven, and tell the stars, if thou be able to number them: and He said unto him, So shall thy seed be"* (Genesis 15:5).

There are no limitations when it comes to God's ability and desire to multiply and increase every area of your life. Deuteronomy 7:9,13,15 (AMPC) says:

> *Know, recognize, and understand therefore that the Lord your God, He is God, the faithful God, Who keeps covenant and steadfast love and mercy with those who love Him and keep His commandments, to a thousand generations . . .*
>
> *And He will love you, bless you, and multiply you; He will also bless the fruit of your body and the fruit of your land, your grain, your new wine, and your oil, the increase of your cattle and the young of your flock in the land which He swore to your fathers to give you . . .*
>
> *And the Lord will take away from you all sickness. . . .*

Moses acknowledged God's promise of increase to the children of Israel and prayed in Deuteronomy 1:11, *"May the Lord, the God of your fathers, make you a thousand times as many as you are and bless you as He has promised you!"*

I don't believe that this promise of increase was only about having a bunch of kids. Parents that are unable to feed, clothe, and provide for their children are miserably heartbroken people. The thousand times increase would have been a curse without an equal increase in wealth to meet their daily needs.

When the children of Israel came out of Egypt, they were happier, healthier, and wealthier than they had ever been in their lives. God gave them silver, gold, and land so that they might observe His statutes and keep His laws.

> *He brought [Israel] forth also with silver and gold, and there was not one feeble person among their tribes . . .*
>
> *He brought forth His people with joy, and His chosen ones with gladness and singing.*
>
> *And gave them the lands of the nations [of Canaan], and they reaped the fruits of those peoples' labor,*
>
> *That they might observe His statutes and keep His laws [hearing, receiving, loving and obeying them]. Praise the Lord! Hallelujah!"*
>
> PSALM 105:37,43-45 (AMPC)

Years ago, I was reading in Exodus 24 about how Moses stood in the presence of God for seven days and seven nights. I had never noticed it before, but it wasn't until after seven days of silence that God spoke to Moses. Exodus 25 begins with, *"And the Lord said . . ."*

I'm certain that Moses was hanging on for that first word from God. What would the Creator impart to him on the smoking Mount Sinai? He must have been listening intently to hear the first words to him from the lips of God. What would they be?

". . . Take for Me an offering . . ."

I don't think Moses said, "What? These people have been slaves for four hundred years without a penny to their name. And now just when they are starting to get ahead, You want me to pass the offering bucket. Are You sure, God?"

Moses, full of thanksgiving to God for delivering the people out of bondage, was obedient to God. The Hebrew children grew up hearing about the principles of giving and receiving. They were ready to be blessed with faithful Abraham and inherit the promise of abundance.

The Bible tells us that those that were of a willing heart brought their offering to God. His plan to start the flow of increase for His children could not begin until they were obedient and wise to sow the seed that was provided by God. Only then could they expect the promise of increase to work for them.

Now some people cringe or get offended when it is offering time. But giving is God's plan to set His people free from lack and bring them into abundance. Just as it was essential to the success of the Hebrew children to have a spirit to give, it is equally important to our success today. Our success is vitally linked to the spirit of giving operating in our life.

There is so much to learn in the Word of God concerning your success. But the most important thing to remember is that you don't have to begin by yourself. God is faithful and He will supply the seed for you to sow. Now don't be foolish and eat your seed! Regardless of how insignificant it may seem to you, when that seed is planted by faith in the fertile soil of God, harvest is on its way.

Just as God sent manna in the wilderness, a raven to feed a prophet, and oil to pay the bills of a destitute widow, He has a plan to multiply you and show you how you can experience good success.

Think About Your Success

Just take a moment right now to think about what you would consider a successful life. Maybe it is simply one that has real joy, perfect peace, and amazing love. Or perhaps you would like a life that is totally free from pain, fear, and lack of any kind. You may have thoughts of the perfect car, house, or job that would make your life better. I want you to realize that you serve a great God that desires to give you all of those things and more.

This is really clear in The Passion Translation of John 10:10: *"A thief has only one thing in mind—he wants to steal, slaughter, and destroy. But I have come to give you everything in abundance, more than you expect —life in its fullness until you overflow!"*

You can take determined steps of faith toward success in your life by making a quality decision to believe this amazing promise. Jesus came to give you everything in abundance—more than you expect. He came so that you could enjoy life in its fullness until you overflow!

I believe that God created us in His image and gave us the force of faith so we can believe Him for the things we desire in this life. Even if others roll their eyes when we declare those things that we're believing God for, we cannot allow them to discourage us from standing firm in our faith. Jeremiah 32:17 declares, *"Ah Lord GOD! behold, Thou hast made the Heaven and the earth by Thy great power and stretched out arm, and there is nothing too hard for Thee."* We must be determined to reject all doubt and embrace the truth that nothing is too hard for our God.

Open the Door to Success

The life that Jesus came to give to you is a supernatural gift that must be received, honored, and valued. Although this message is available for everyone on earth, it is up to each one of us to accept it by faith. Revelation 3:20 says, *"Behold, I stand at the door, and knock: if any man hear My voice, and open the door, I will come in to him, and will sup with him, and he with Me."*

Several years ago, this verse became so real to me during a worship service at our church. I thought about how earnestly Jesus stands at the door to our hearts just waiting for us to welcome Him into every area of our lives. I realized in a much stronger way that it is up to us to open the door—He will not barge in uninvited. However, when we fling open that door and joyfully invite Him into our hearts, we can begin to see that we are suited for success.

Times of Refreshing

I know that it is really easy to let the day-to-day issues of life steal our time with God. I know the thief is always working to kill our dreams and destroy our life. Whenever we find ourselves caught up in his trap, it is up to us to change our ways. God knows exactly what will make our lives better.

This new life that we have in God must not be allowed to stagnate; it must be continually refreshed by the presence of the Lord. Acts 3:19 says, *"Repent ye therefore, and be converted, that your sins may be blotted out, when the times of refreshing shall come from the presence of the Lord."*

I think it is so important to realize that faith comes—it doesn't stack up. Romans 10:17 tells us, *"So then faith **cometh by hearing, and hearing by the Word of God.**"* So, when we hear God's Word, it imparts faith and life into our spirits. In John 6:63, Jesus said, *"It is the Spirit that quickeneth; the flesh profiteth nothing: the words that I speak unto you, they are spirit, and they are life."* Hearing God's Word is the most important thing that you can do to enjoy a life of success.

CHAPTER 11

Beware of the
DREAM KILLERS

Have you ever shared your dream with the wrong person? You may still cringe at the memory of their harsh words or mocking laughter as you told them about the deepest hope of your heart. That's a dream killer. Although they may not have realized it, they were being used by the devil to rob God's promise from your heart and stop the fulfillment of your dream. That is why you must become wise to the works of the devil and be aware of his tactics.

I want you to realize that dreams never have an expiration date. God has not given up on your dream, and neither should you. Even if your dream has been aborted, God is ready to resurrect it and breathe life into it once again. No matter how unbelievable your dreams may seem to others, you need to realize today that this is your time to receive your dream. It is time to get stirred up and believe everything that God wants to accomplish in your life.

You can walk in divine healing and prosperity. Your loved ones can be saved, and love can be restored into your home. You may have a dream of owning your own business that is yet to be fulfilled. Or it may be that God has placed a call to the ministry on your life and it is still in the dream stage. Regardless of what is in your heart, God desires for you to attain every promise in His Word so that your dreams will be fulfilled. Isaiah 55:8-11 says,

> *For My thoughts are not your thoughts, neither are your ways My ways, saith the LORD.*
>
> *For as the heavens are higher than the earth, so are My ways higher than your ways, and My thoughts than your thoughts.*
>
> *For as the rain cometh down, and the snow from heaven, and returneth not thither, but watereth the earth, and maketh it bring forth and bud, that it **may give seed** to the sower, and bread to the eater:*
>
> ***So shall My word** be that goeth forth out of My mouth: it shall not return unto Me void, but it shall accomplish that which I please, and it shall prosper in the thing whereto I sent it.*

In the above passage of scripture, the prophet Isaiah compared God's way of operation to a seed. God wanted us to understand the way He operates. When God speaks His Word from His mouth, it is never void or without power of fulfillment. That is how the world was created. He sent His Word and expected it to succeed and accomplish results, and so should you.

I believe that every dream from God began as a seed from God's mouth to the soil of your heart. Isaiah made it clear that that's exactly how God gets His thoughts into the earth.

Since you were created in His image and in His likeness, He expects you to operate on this earth in the same way as He does. Your dream of success may still be in the seed stage, but it will never grow to maturity until you begin to speak it out of your mouth.

Jesus taught this seed principle in Mark 4:30-32:

> *And He said, Whereunto shall we liken the kingdom of God? or with what comparison shall we compare it?*
>
> *It is like a grain of mustard seed, which, when it is sown in the earth, is less than all the seeds that be in the earth:*
>
> ***But when it is sown, it groweth up, and becometh greater than all herbs, and shooteth out great branches; so that the fowls of the air may lodge under the shadow of it.***

The kingdom of God operates on the principle of the seed being sown, growing up, becoming greater, and shooting out in every direction. Understanding this principle of the seed is critical to your success. In fact, when explaining the parable of the seed in Mark 4, Jesus told His disciples that if they didn't know this, then they couldn't know anything about God's way of doing things.

> *And He began again to teach by the sea side: and there was gathered unto Him a great multitude, so that He entered into a ship, and sat in the sea; and the whole multitude was by the sea on the land.*
>
> *And He taught them many things by parables, and said unto them in His doctrine,*
>
> *Hearken; Behold, there went out a sower to sow:*
>
> *And it came to pass, as he sowed, some fell by the way side, and the fowls of the air came and devoured it up.*
>
> *And some fell on stony ground, where it had not much earth; and immediately it sprang up, because it had no depth of earth:*

> *But when the sun was up, it was scorched; and because it had no root, it withered away.*
>
> *And some fell among thorns, and the thorns grew up, and choked it, and it yielded no fruit.*
>
> *And other fell on good ground, and did yield fruit that sprang up and increased; and brought forth, some thirty, and some sixty, and some an hundred.*
>
> *And He said unto them, He that hath ears to hear, let him hear.*
>
> *And when He was alone, they that were about Him with the twelve asked of Him the parable.*
>
> *And He said unto them, Unto you it is given to know the mystery of the kingdom of God: but unto them that are without, all these things are done in parables:*
>
> *That seeing they may see, and not perceive; and hearing they may hear, and not understand; lest at any time they should be converted, and their sins should be forgiven them.*
>
> *And He said unto them, Know ye not this parable? and how then will ye know all parables?*
>
> Mark 4:1-13

In this passage, Jesus revealed three things that will stop our seeds from producing fruit in our lives. I call them dream killers.

Dream Killer #1: Doubt

This dream killer should be very familiar to us because the devil does not have any new tricks. He tried this one on Adam and Eve in the garden and doubt robbed them of their garden home and their God-given authority.

> *Now the serpent was more subtil than any beast of the field which the LORD God had made. And he said unto the woman, Yea, hath God said, Ye shall not eat of every tree of the garden?*

And the woman said unto the serpent, We may eat of the fruit of the trees of the garden:

But of the fruit of the tree which is in the midst of the garden, God hath said, Ye shall not eat of it, neither shall ye touch it, lest ye die.

And the serpent said unto the woman, Ye shall not surely die:

For God doth know that in the day ye eat thereof, then your eyes shall be opened, and ye shall be as gods, knowing good and evil.

And when the woman saw that the tree was good for food, and that it was pleasant to the eyes, and a tree to be desired to make one wise, she took of the fruit thereof, and did eat, and gave also unto her husband with her; and he did eat.

And the eyes of them both were opened, and they knew that they were naked; and they sewed fig leaves together, and made themselves aprons.

And they heard the voice of the LORD God walking in the garden in the cool of the day: and Adam and his wife hid themselves from the presence of the LORD God amongst the trees of the garden.

And the LORD God called unto Adam, and said unto him, Where art thou?

And he said, I heard Thy voice in the garden, and I was afraid, because I was naked; and I hid myself.

And He said, Who told thee that thou wast naked? Hast thou eaten of the tree, whereof I commanded thee that thou shouldest not eat?

And the man said, The woman whom Thou gavest to be with me, she gave me of the tree, and I did eat.

And the LORD God said unto the woman, What is this that thou hast done? And the woman said, The serpent beguiled me, and I did eat.

And the LORD God said unto the serpent, Because thou hast done this, thou art cursed above all cattle, and above every *beast of the field; upon thy belly shalt thou go, and dust shalt thou eat all the days of thy life:*

And I will put enmity between thee and the woman, and between thy seed and her seed; it shall bruise thy head, and thou shalt bruise His heel.

Unto the woman He said, I will greatly multiply thy sorrow and thy conception; in sorrow thou shalt bring forth children; and thy desire shall be to thy husband, and he shall rule over thee.

And unto Adam He said, Because thou hast hearkened unto the voice of thy wife, and hast eaten of the tree, of which I commanded thee, saying, Thou shalt not eat of it: cursed is the ground for thy sake; in sorrow shalt thou eat of it all the days of thy life;

Thorns also and thistles shall it bring forth to thee; and thou shalt eat the herb of the field;

In the sweat of thy face shalt thou eat bread, till thou return unto the ground; for out of it wast thou taken: for dust thou art, and unto dust shalt thou return.

GENESIS 3:1-19

Although Satan succeeded in killing God's dream for mankind with the first Adam, the second Adam (Jesus) did not fall into his trap.

And Jesus being full of the Holy Ghost returned from Jordan, and was led by the Spirit into the wilderness,

Being forty days tempted of the devil. And in those days He did eat nothing: and when they were ended, He afterward hungered.

And the devil said unto Him, If thou be the Son of God, command this stone that it be made bread.

And Jesus answered him, saying, It is written, That man shall not live by bread alone, but by every Word of God.

> *And the devil, taking Him up into an high mountain, shewed unto Him all the kingdoms of the world in a moment of time.*
>
> *And the devil said unto Him, All this power will I give Thee, and the glory of them: for that is delivered unto me; and to whomsoever I will I give it.*
>
> *If Thou therefore wilt worship me, all shall be Thine.*
>
> *And Jesus answered and said unto him, Get thee behind Me, Satan: for it is written, Thou shalt worship the Lord thy God, and Him only shalt thou serve.*
>
> *And he brought Him to Jerusalem, and set Him on a pinnacle of the temple, and said unto Him, If thou be the Son of God, cast Thyself down from hence:*
>
> *For it is written, He shall give His angels charge over Thee, to keep Thee:*
>
> *And in their hands they shall bear Thee up, lest at any time Thou dash thy foot against a stone.*
>
> *And Jesus answering said unto him, It is said, Thou shalt not tempt the Lord thy God.*
>
> *And when the devil had ended all the temptation, he departed from Him for a season.*
>
> LUKE 4:1-13

If the devil will go after Jesus, what makes you think he will hesitate to go after you to kill your dream? In His encounter with the devil in the wilderness, Jesus demonstrated how you can stop the devil by declaring God's Word from your heart and defeat the dream killer called doubt.

In His parable of the sower, Jesus wanted us to recognize that once God's Word is sown into our heart, the devil comes immediately to take away the Word by planting his words of doubt.

> *And these are they by the way side, where the Word is sown; but when they have heard, Satan cometh immediately, and **taketh away the Word** that was sown in their hearts.*
>
> MARK 4:15

The devil does not want any of God's children to be healthy or successful. He wants to keep us sick and in debt. He may try to sound theological, but his only motive is to kill our dreams and stop God's promise from coming to pass.

Years ago, Jesse and I didn't understand that we couldn't tell our dreams to just anyone. Sometimes people tried to kill our dreams with their doubt. Maybe it was too big for them to grasp, but then again, it wasn't their dream; it was ours.

When Jesse told a pastor that God said our ministry would one day have a jet to spread the Gospel of Jesus Christ to the world, that man laughed in his face. He shook his head and told him, "You will never get a jet. You don't have enough money to put gas in your little Toyota!" That man was looking at what he could see, but Jesse was looking at God's promise. He refused to allow that man or anyone else to kill our dream by planting seeds of doubt.

Years later, that pastor contacted us after hearing that we had purchased our first ministry jet. When he asked for a ride on the plane, Jesse told him, "No. I won't let doubt and unbelief get on my plane!" Jesse and I know that our dreams are too big for some people, but it doesn't stop us from declaring God's promise to us. We refuse to let anyone kill our dreams with doubt.

Dream Killer #2: Offense

Once the first dream killer of doubt has taken away God's Word from your heart, the next killer will be offense.

> *And these are they likewise which are sown on stony ground; who, when they have heard the Word, immediately receive it with gladness;*

> *And have no root in themselves, and so endure but for a time: afterward, when affliction or persecution ariseth for the Word's sake, immediately they are **offended**.*
>
> MARK 4:16-17

Some people think they have a right to be offended. They don't realize that this is a tactic of the devil to kill their dream and rob them of God's promise. But offense is a killer of dreams. If they allow it to take hold of their heart, it will rob every bit of joy, peace, and hope for success from their life.

In the early years of our ministry, Jesse had many opportunities to get offended. Several pastors stole the offerings that people designated for our ministry, yet he kept going back to their churches. I was not as forgiving as Jesse, and it irritated me to see him accept invitations from those pastors. When I asked Jesse why he went back, he told me that he refused to be offended and his concern was only for the people that would be ministered to during the meetings. Today, Jesse has ministered in thousands of different churches since he began preaching in 1976. He is loved the world over because he refused to allow a few corrupt pastors to kill his dream to preach the Gospel to the world.

Dream Killer #3: Cares of this World

Several years ago, Jesse and I spent some time with an elderly couple. During our conversation, they shared their disappointment about not having seen the fulfillment of their dream. When they were young, they knew that God had called them to preach the Gospel, but they never felt that there was a convenient time to step out. The more they talked, Jesse and I could clearly see why they were frustrated so late in their life. Over the years, they made decisions that pulled them off course and away from their dream. The cares of this world came in and literally choked the Word of God about their calling right out of their heart.

> *And these are they which are sown among thorns; such as hear the Word,*
> *And the cares of this world, and the deceitfulness of riches, and the lusts of other things entering in,* **choke the Word,** *and it becometh unfruitful.*
>
> Mark 4:18-19

Dreams sent by God will never be fulfilled if your heart is shallow and crowded with the cares of this world. You need to get rooted in God's Word so that you can grow and become fruitful. No root equals no fruit.

Once you establish your heart on God's Word, you will still need to stay sharp and continually guard against things that will choke the life out of your dream. Determine today to get rooted in God's Word so that no devil from hell can kill your dream.

The Word of God: A Dream Accomplisher

God's Word has supernatural power to produce life to all those that hear it and receive it. Mark 4:20 goes on to say:

> *And these are they which are sown on good ground; such as hear the Word, and receive it, and bring forth fruit, some thirtyfold, some sixty, and some an hundred.*

This hundredfold promise of Jesus belongs to those who will receive it by faith. Refuse to limit God's blessing in your life and you will successfully accomplish every dream that He has placed on your heart.

> *Therefore, my dear ones, as you have always obeyed [my suggestions], so now, not only [with the enthusiasm you would show] in my presence but much more because I am absent, work out (cultivate, carry out to the goal, and fully complete) your own salvation with reverence and awe and trembling (self-distrust, with serious caution, tenderness of conscience, watchfulness against temptation, timidly shrinking from whatever might offend God and discredit the name of Christ).*
>
> *[Not in your own strength] for it is God Who is all the while effectually at work in you [energizing and creating in you the power and desire], both to will and to work for His good pleasure and satisfaction and delight.*
>
> PHILIPPIANS 2:12-13 (AMPC)

Each time you hear God's Word, you are being energized with seeds of faith by the Holy Ghost. God is working in you now and creating in you the power to accomplish every dream that He has placed on your heart.

I want to help you recognize the three basic stages toward dream fulfillment: conception, perception, and reception. The first stage is when the dream is conceived in your heart. Then, once a dream is conceived, it must be perceived. This second stage will require extensive time with God in His Word so that you can fully understand the vision and the steps that will propel you toward the fulfillment of your dream. When you are obedient to follow those steps, you will move into the third stage, which is reception.

Never make apologies for the size of your dream. Just one God-related thought has the power to bring you out of lack and into abundance. I heard about a Christian woman in Texas who had a thought to produce chocolates to look like tiny hot tamales. Jesse brought home a palm-sized wooden crate full of those delicious chocolates from a meeting one night. Now I am sure that the dream killers came by this lady's house more than once, but they could not stop her. She was determined to succeed. I heard that she made millions of dollars from that one thought. Once a dream is conceived and perceived, it will be received.

Every success story you will ever hear about began as a thought or a seed in the soil of someone's heart. It can happen to you, too! So, stay in faith and refuse to allow the dream killers of doubt, offense, and the cares of this world to steal the seeds of God's Word from your heart. Stay suited for success and you will accomplish the dreams that God has placed in your heart.

SUITED FOR SUCCESS

PRAYER OF SALVATION

If you are at the point in your life where you are ready to make a personal commitment to follow Christ, all you have to do is reach out to Him now in prayer. He is listening and waiting to come into your heart and help you live a successful life. Will you invite Him in right now? If you'd like to pray and receive Christ as your Savior, you can use this simple prayer as a guide:

> *"Lord Jesus, I ask You to come into my life and forgive me of all my sins. I confess my sins before You this day. I denounce Satan and all his works. I confess Jesus as the Lord of my life. Thank You for saving me. I believe with my heart and I confess with my mouth that You rose from the dead. I am saved. Write my name in the Lamb's Book of Life. Today is my Godday with the Lord Jesus! I pray this prayer to the Father in the name of Jesus. Amen."*

If you just prayed this prayer, please let me know by using the contact information in this book or by going to www.jdm.org. I'd like to pray for you and send you a free booklet, called *Understanding Salvation*, to help you understand a little more about this new life in Christ. Congratulations and welcome to the family of God!

—Cathy

ABOUT THE AUTHOR

Reverend Cathy Duplantis is an anointed teacher of the Gospel who is dedicated to living by faith and inspiring others to do the same. Cathy is the wife of Evangelist Jesse Duplantis and has worked continually with her husband in ministry since it began in 1976, serving as Administrator, Editor in Chief of *Voice of the Covenant* magazine, and television co-host.

Cathy uses her life experiences and divinely given revelations to encourage and inspire her audience and is a favorite guest speaker for women's conferences and church meetings. She also is continuing to preach the Gospel with Jesse in meetings throughout the USA.

Along with her husband, Cathy is the co-founder of Covenant Church, a local outreach of JDM in the greater New Orleans area. It was her vision to build a church where people would be encouraged to realize their potential in Christ Jesus, to be able to overcome life's circumstances, and to experience success spiritually, emotionally, and physically. In the summer of 2017 Cathy obeyed God and stepped into the Senior Pastor position of Covenant Church. Now not only is she sharing the Gospel through her local church, but she is continuing to spread the love of Jesus around the world. Cathy desires to show believers everywhere how they can be transformed into powerful and joyful people of faith by applying the teachings found in God's Word.

OTHER BOOKS
by Cathy Duplantis

How to Behave in a Cave

Keeping a Clean Heart
(Mini-Book)

The Healing Word
(Book and CD)

The Peaceful Word
(Book and CD)

The Prosperous Word
(Book and CD)

You Are Designed for Glorious Living

OTHER CONTENT

Other ministry resources by Cathy Duplantis are available through **www.jdm.org** and the JDM App (**Total.JDM.org**).

CONTACT US

To contact Jesse Duplantis Ministries with prayer requests, praise reports, comments, or to schedule Cathy Duplantis at your church, conference, or seminar, please write, call, or email:

> Jesse Duplantis Ministries
> PO Box 1089
> Destrehan, LA 70047
> 985-764-2000
> www.jdm.org

We also invite you to connect with us on social media:

Facebook:	/JesseDuplantisMinistries
Twitter:	@jesse_duplantis
Instagram:	@jesseduplantisministries
YouTube:	/jesseduplantisministries
Pinterest:	/JesseDuplantisMinistries
TikTok:	@jesseduplantisministries